Gold 916·6 (22 carat)	
Gold 750 (18 carat)	
Gold 585 (14 carat)	
Gold 375 (9 carat)	
Silver 958·4 (Britannia)	
Silver 925 (Sterling)	
Platinum 950	

1. Look for the Hallmark .. *it's your* extremely accurate analyses which are normally carried out on small samples removed from the articles before they *Safeguard*

have been finally polished.

British Hallmarks

What information do hallmarks give?

British hallmarks have acted as a safeguard to purchasers of **The Sponsor's Mark** indicates the manufacturer or sponsor gold and silver articles for over six centuries. Hallmarking is of the article. In Britain the mark consists of the initials of the still one of the most important forms of consumer protection person or firm and where two or more sponsors have the and in 1975 was extended to include platinum. The same initials, there is a variation in the surrounding shield or consumer benefits in many ways. For example, it is an style of letters.

offence for any trader to sell or describe an article as gold, silver or platinum unless it has been hallmarked. (There are **The Standard Mark** denotes that the precious metal content some exceptions, for example gold articles weighing less of the alloy from which the article is made is not less than than one gram, silver articles weighing less than 7.78 grams the standard indicated.

and platinum articles weighing less than half a gram. Certain specific items are exempt if made before 1975, such as The diagram below shows the legal standards and the stone set gold rings and platinum articles, also all articles minimum content of precious metal by weight in parts per made before 1900). The following questions and answers thousand.

will help you to understand the hallmarking system.

Why do I need protection? Pure gold, silver and platinum are too soft to be used in jewellery or domestic articles and are normally alloyed with other metals. This lowers the intrinsic value and also raises the question of how much other metal has been added. It is impossible to tell what proportion of precious metal there is in any article withoutthe help of chemical analysis. Colour alone is no guide, even brass can look like gold -especially if it has been plated with gold.

How do hallmarks protect me? Hallmarks on an article show that it has been tested at an official Assay Office and they certify that the metal used conforms to one of the legal standards of fineness or purity. The Assay Offices in Britain are incorporated by royal charter or by statute and all are independent of any trade organisation. The tests are 2

3

3

The Assay Office Mark identifies the particular office at which the article was tested and marked. There are now four **British Articles**

British Assay Offices-in London, Birmingham, Sheffield and Edinburgh. There were other Assay Offices in former times.

The Date Letter shows the year in which the article was **Prior to**

Standard

From 1975

1975

hallmarked.

How can I recognise hallmarks? Hallmarking was first instituted as long ago as 1300. The designs of individual 22 carat

gold

marks have changed from time to time and new marks have Marked in

been added. It is impossible in a small booklet to show all England

the hallmarks which you may come across, but the Marked in

illustrations on the following pages should help you to Scotland

identify most of them. After 1st January 1975 all four British Assay Offices use the same date letter, but to date earlier pieces

4

you will first have to identify the Assay Office mark before turning to the appropriate list. Date letters for the 18 carat

gold

existing Assay Offices are given in this booklet. The marks
Marked in

shown are those used on silver; the same letters are used England

on gold, but before 1975 the surrounding shields may differ.

Marked in

Earlier cycles of letters and those for Assay Offices which
Scotland

have closed can be found in more comprehensive publications.
Here is an example of a complete hallmark.

14 carat

gold

9 carat

gold

It shows the sponsor's mark, followed by the mark for sterling silver, the London Assay Office mark and the date letter for 1976.

Sterling

silver

Marked in

England

2. STANDARD MARK

4

5

gold & Sterling silver Britannia silver

gold, silver &
platinum

gold   silver

gold &   silver
platinum

gold   silver

gold, silver &
platinum

Britannia silver

Marked in

Scotland

Platinum

Britannia

silver

Platinum

3. ASSAY OFFICE MARK

British Articles

Imported Articles

Prior to 1975

Assay Office

From 1975

22 carat gold

London

18 carat gold

14 carat gold

Birmingham

9 carat gold

Sheffield

Sterling silver

6

7

gold & silver

gold & silver

Assay Office

From 1975

Edinburgh

Gold & silver

London

unchanged

Notes - (i) Some variations in the surrounding shields are found before 1975. (ii) All Assay Offices mark Britannia silver, but only London (prior to 1975) had a special Assay Office mark for this standard.

unchanged

Birmingham

Imported Articles

Assay Office

Prior to 1975

Sheffield

unchanged

gold

silver

Edinburgh

unchanged

London

Here are some of the other marks which you may find on gold or silver articles.

Birmingham

Former Assay Office Marks. Several of the larger provincial cities had Assay Offices which are now closed.

Sheffield

Each had its distinctive mark, some of the more important of which are shown below. There is also an Assay Office in Dublin and marks struck there before 1 st April 1923 are recognised as approved British hallmarks. The Dublin mark Edinburgh

is a figure of Hibernia.

8

9

Chester

Dublin

Glasgow

Newcastle

Exeter

George III

Victoria

Silver Jubilee
1935

Coronation
1953

Silver Jubilee
1977

4. CONVENTION HALLMARKS

From 1st June 1976 special marks applied at authorised Assay
Offices in the United Kingdom, Austria, Finland, Sweden and
Switzerland are legally recognised as approved hallmarks under an
International Convention. The marks consist of a *Sponsor's Mark*,
a *Common Control Mark,* a *Fineness Mark* (arabic numerals

showing the standard in parts per thousand), and *an Assay Office Mark.* There is no date letter.

Duty Marks. Between 1784 and 1890 an excise duty on Convention marks recognised in the United Kingdom are gold and silver articles was collected by the Assay Offices illustrated below. The Sponsor's mark and Assay Office and a mark depicting the Sovereign's head was struck to mark are not shown.

show that it had been paid. These are two examples.

Precious Metal

Common

Fineness

Control

Mark

Mark

Gold

18

750

carat

Commemorative Marks. There are three other marks to commemorate special events, the Silver Jubilee of King George V and Queen Mary in 1935, the Coronation of 14

585

Queen Elizabeth II in 1953 and her Silver Jubilee in 1977.

carat

10

11

9 carat

375

Silver

Sterling

925

1679

Platinum

950

1680

Marks for silver of 800 and 830 standard are also included in the Convention, but these are not approved legal standards for articles sold in Britain.

1681

Marking in Other Countries. In many foreign countries the only marks used on precious metal articles are those struck by the manufacturer. These do not, of course, indicate the 1682

independent certification and consequent protection afforded by British or Convention hallmarks.

1683

5. LONDON

1684

1685

1678

12

13

1686

1694

1687

1695

1688

1696

1689

1690

1697

1691

1698

1692

1699

1693

1700

14

15

1701

1709

1702

1710

1703

1711

1712

1704

1713

1705

1706

1714

1707

1715

1708

1716

16

17

1717

1718

1725

1719

1726

1727

1720

1728

1721

1722

1729

1723

1730

1724

1731

18

19

1732

1739

1733

1740

1734

1741

1735

1742

1736

1743

1737

1744

1738

1745

1739

1746

1747

20

21

1748

1756

1749

1757

1750

1758

1759

1751

1760

1752

1761

1753

1762

1754

1763

1755

1764

22

23

1765

1775

1766

1776

1767

1777

1768

1778

1769

1779

1770

1780

1771

1781

1772

1782

1773

1783

1774

24

25

p

 q

 r

 s

 t

 u

 A

B

C

D

1791

1784

1792

1793

1785

1794

1786

1795

1787

1796

1788

1797

1789

1798

1799

1790

26

27

(L)

(M)

(N)

(O)

(P)

(Q)

(R)

(S)

(T)

(U)

(a)

(b)

1800

1809

1801

1810

1802

1811

1803

1812

1804

1813

1805

1814

1806

1815

1807

1816

1808

1817

28

29

ⓘ

ⓚ

ⓛ

ⓜ

ⓝ

ⓞ

ⓟ

ⓠ

ⓡ

ⓢ

36

1818

1826

1819

1827

1820

1828

1821

1829

1830

1822

1831

1823

1832

1833

1824

1825

30

31

1834

1842

1835

1843

1836

1844

1837

1845

1846

1847

1838

1848

1839

1849

1840

1850

1841

1851

32

33

1852

1861

1853

1862

1854

1863

1855

1834

1856

1865

1857

1866

1858

1867

1859

1868

1860

1869

34

35

1870

1879

1871

1880

1872

1881

1873

1882

1874

1883

1875

1884

1876

1885

1877

1886

1878

1887

36

37

1888

1889

1896

1890

1897

1898

1891

1899

1892

1900

1893

1901

1894

1902

1895

38

39

1903

1912

1904

1913

1905

1914

1906

1915

1907

1908

1916

1909

1917

1910

1918

1911

40

41

1919

1926

1920

1927

1921

1928

1922

1929

1930

1931

1923

1932

1924

1933

1925

1934

42

43

1935

1942

1943

1944

1936

1937

1945

1938

1946

1947

1939

1948

1940

1949

1941

1950

44

45

b

c

d

e

f

g

h

i

k

l

m

1951

1960

1952

1961

1953

1962

1954

1963

1955

1964

1956

1965

1957

1966

1958

1967

1959

46

47

1968

1975

1969

1976

1970

1977

1978

1971

1979

1972

1973

6. BIRMINGHAM

1974

48

49

1773

1780

1774

1781

1775

1782

1776

1783

1777

1778

1784

1779

1785

50

51

1792

1786

1793

1787

1794

1788

1795

1789

1796

1790

1797

1791

1798

52

53

e

 f

 g

 h

 i

 j

 k

 l

 m

 n

 o

1799

1806

1800

1807

1801

1808

1809

1802

1803

1810

1804

1811

1812

1805

54

55

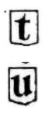

1813

1820

1814

1821

1815

1822

1816

1823

1817

1824

1818

1825

1826

1819

56

57

1827

1828

1834

1829

1835

1830

1836

1831

1837

1832

1838

1833

58

59

1839

1846

1840

1847

1841

1848

1842

1843

1849

1850

1844

1851

1845

60

61

1852

1859

1853

1860

1854

1861

1855

1862

1863

1856

1834

1857

1865

1858

62

63

1866

1873

1867

1874

1868

1869

1875

1870

1876

1871

1877

1872

1878

64

65

1879

1886

1880

1887

1881

1888

1882

1889

1883

1890

1884

1885

1891

66

67

1892

1899

1893

1900

1894

1901

1895

1902

1896

1903

1897

1904

1898

68

69

1905

1912

1906

1913

1907

1914

1908

1915

1909

1916

1910

1917

1911

1918

70

71

1919

1926

1920

1927

1921

1928

1922

1929

1923

1930

1924

1931

1925

1932

72

73

1933

1940

1934

1941

1935

1942

1936

1943

1937

1944

1938

1945

1939

1946

74

75

1947

1953

1948

1954

1955

1949

1956

1957

1950

1958

1951

1959

1952

76

77

1960

1967

1961

1968

1962

1969

1963

1970

1964

1971

1965

1972

1966

78

79

1973

1978

1979

1974

7. SHEFFIELD

1975

1773

1976

1774

1977

1775

80

81

1776

1783

1777

1784

1778

1785

1779

1780

1786

1781

1787

1782

82

83

1788

1795

1789

1796

1790

1797

1791

1798

1792

1799

1793

1800

1794

1801

84

85

1802

1809

1803

1810

1804

1811

1805

1812

1806

1813

1807

1814

1808

1815

86

87

1816

1823

1817

1824

1818

1825

1819

1826

1820

1827

1821

1828

1822

1829

88

89

1830

1836

1831

1837

1832

1838

1833

1839

1834

1840

1835

1841

90

91

1842

1849

1843

1850

1844

1851

1852

1845

1853

1846

1854

1847

1855

1848

92

93

1856

1863

1857

1834

1858

1865

1859

1866

1860

1867

1861

1868

1862

94

95

1869

1876

1870

1877

1871

1878

1872

1879

1873

1880

1874

1881

1875

1882

96

97

1883

1890

1884

1885

1891

1886

1892

1887

1893

1888

1894

1889

1895

98

99

1896

1903

1897

1904

1898

1905

1906

1899

1907

1900

1908

1901

1902

1909

100

101

106

1910

1916

1911

1917

1912

1913

1918

1919

1914

1920

1915

1921

102

103

1922

1929

1923

1930

1924

1931

1932

1925

1933

1926

1927

1934

1928

1935

104

105

1936

1943

1937

1944

1938

1945

1939

1946

1940

1947

1941

1948

1942

1949

106

107

1950

1957

1951

1958

1952

1959

1953

1960

1954

1961

1955

1962

1956

1963

108

109

1964

1971

1965

1972

1966

1973

1967

1974

1968

1969

1975

1970

1976

110

111

1977

1706

1978

1707

1979

1708

1709

Between 1780/1853, the Crown and Date letter are usually enclosed in the same shield on small articles.

8. EDINBURGH

1710

1711

1705

1712

112

113

1713

1720

1714

1721

1715

1722

1723

1716

1724

1717

1725

1718

1726

1719

1727

114

115

1728

1735

1729

1736

1730

1737

1731

1738

1732

1739

1733

1740

1734

1741

116

117

1742

1749

1743

1750

1744

1751

1752

1745

1753

1746

1754

1747

1755

1748

118

119

1756

1762

1757

1763

1758

1764

1765

1759

1766

1760

1767

1761

1768

120

121

—

1769

1776

1770

1777

1771

1778

1772

1779

1773

1780

1781

1774

1782

1775

122

123

1783

1789

1790

1784

1791

1785

1792

1793

1786

1794

1787

1795

1788

124

125

1796

1803

1797

1804

1798

1805

1799

1806

1800

1807

1808

1801

1809

1802

126

127

1810

1817

1811

1818

1812

1819

1813

1820

1814

1821

1815

1822

1816

1823

128

129

1824

1832

1825

1833

1826

1834

1827

1835

1828

1836

1829

1837

1830

1838

1831

130

131

1839

1846

1840

1847

1848

1841

1849

1842

1850

1843

1851

1844

1852

1845

132

133

1853

1860

1854

1861

1855

1862

1856

1863

1857

1834

1858

1865

1859

1866

134

135

1881

1888

1882

1889

1883

1890

1884

1885

1891

1886

1892

1887

1893

138

139

1894

1901

1895

1902

1896

1903

1897

1904

1898

1905

1899

1906

1907

1900

140

141

1908

1915

1909

1916

1910

1917

1911

1918

1912

1919

1913

1920

1914

1921

142

143

1922

1929

1923

1930

1924

1931

1925

1932

1926

1933

1927

1934

1935

1928

144

145

1936

1943

1937

1944

1938

1945

1939

1946

1940

1947

1941

1948

1942

1949

146

147

1950

1957

1951

1958

1952

1959

1953

1960

1954

1961

1955

1962

1963

1956

148

149

1964

1971

1965

1972

1966

1973-4

1967

1968

1975

1969

1976

1970

1977

150

151

1978

1979

152

Printed in Great Britain
by Amazon

38943306R00088